FILL IN THE ST...

(the origi...

This **book** is an ...
to a series cal...
Providing a **taste** of que...ions and **prompts**
made entirely in **your favor**.
The pages and **illustrations** range
from very funny to **somewhat serious**,
accompanied by rhymes that are
informative yet minutely **mysterious**.
Each **book** in the series has
its own unique and **focused theme**,
created for different mindsets,
ambitions and **dreams**.

WARNING: contains pages with spaces.

Fill in the Space

Written and Created by Sally Safadi
3rd Edition 2015

Published by **Neurons Away LLC**
Syracuse. New York

Printed at
Quartier Printing
5795 Bridge Street
E. Syracuse. NY 13057

First Printing (FROM THE SKY) 2014
Second Printing. (FILL IN THE SPACE) 2014

ISBN: 978-1-943825-01-1

NeuronsAway.com

Hey there.

Have you ever really thought
about you and this world
and all the things you've been taught?

Have you ever stopped to question
where does life go?
Is it true what you have been told
and what you think you know?

Is this really a reality?
Or maybe some kind of dandy dream?
All these questions at once.
overwhelming they may seem.

Eventually the answers
will be as clear as the sun
but for now we shall begin
by going one by one.

Let me go ahead
and briefly explain
this book is craftily created
to stimulate your brain.

This idea may appear to be
somewhat unusual and strange.
However. if you follow along
you will notice your world change.

Right now
you are only Neurons Away.
from a whole new realm
made for creation and play.

Enjoy the moment
and ponder on through
take the chance to
imagine something new.

what is SPACE?

what will you do before you go?

what will you take with you?

what will you discover?

YOU HAVE A TRIP INTO SPACE

DESIGN YOUR SPACESHIP

Write Some questions you

don't know the answers to.

Pick something (anything) and DRAW (or describe) it from many different angles

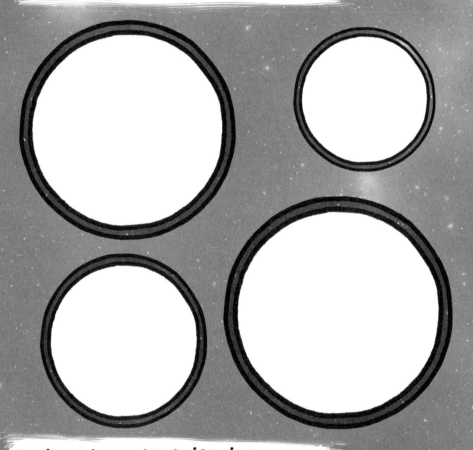

By **observing** or **experiencing** something from different **perspectives**, you gain a **better understanding** of it, allowing you to effectively meet your **objectives**. Be it an **item**, a **relationship** or some sort of **work task**, it's **good** to **view** it from **all around** even if **you** must **ask**.

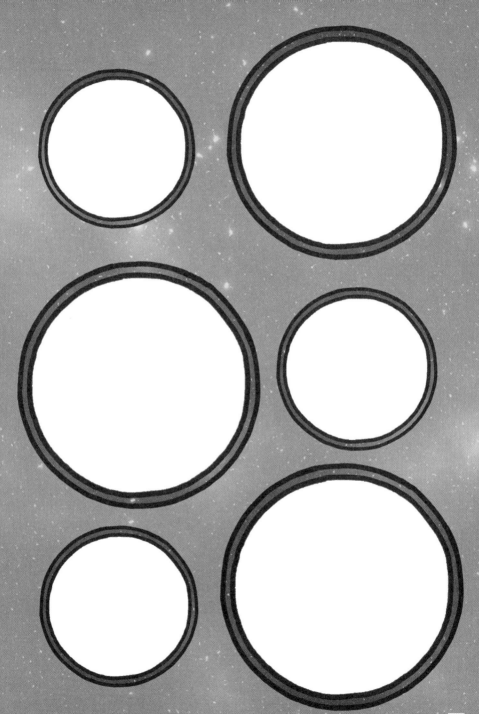

It is expected that over
time our bodies **adapt** and **grow**
to **become more capable** in our
practical **lives**, this we **all know.**
But how and when do we
emotionally and **consciously** mature?
That may be a **question** we may
 unlikely know **for sure.**

When exactly does a child

become an adult?

show description:

name your cartoon show:

character description:

write something your cartoon character would say:

Draw yourself as cartoon character.

Don't be
fooled by
your
reality,
this
world is
strictly
make-
believe.

What are you made up of?

Your **existence** is definitely
something to be in **awe of**.
Like that **feeling** you get when
looking at the **star**-filled **sky** above.
These pages are here
to **discover** and **inform**
that you, my beloved,
are a **miracle**
in **flesh** and in **form**.

What do you **imagine**
every one is doing?
What kind of life
is each **pursuing?**
So many lives all
happening at once.
Every one living
their own experience.

Draw what's **happening** in each **window**

dRaW the cOOLeST eLePHant

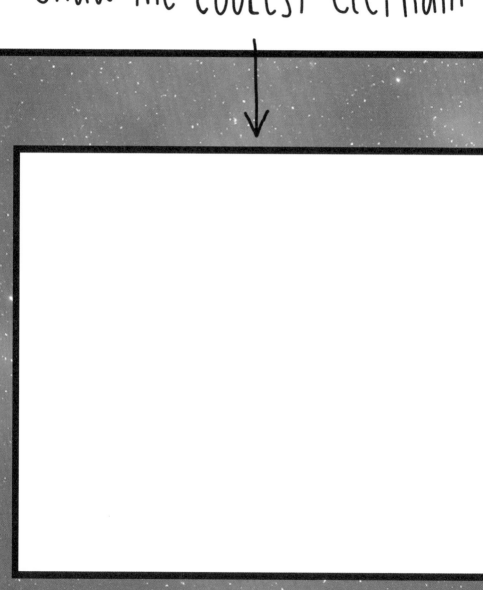

what's cooler than the coolest elephant?

List
ALL
the
SOUNDS
you

Notice your **attention shift**
and **sift** from the **ceiling** to the **floor.**
That background **chatter** becomes
what **you're** listening for.

Doing an exercise like this **each day**
will **increase** your sense of **awareness**
and even **possibly** advance
your **mental alertness.**

CaN
heaR
Right
Now

Fill this bottle with what's good for you

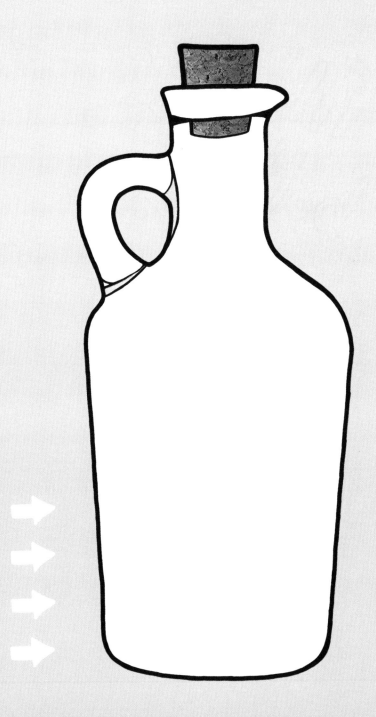

Maps are **created** and **used**,
as **essential** and defining tools.

They **guide** and direct the way,
Through this **wondrous** world as **we play**.

You can add names, **trees**, seas and bees
Maybe even some **hemp** factories.

CREATE the map the
way you want it to be.

List ten and a half words you enjoy

think of words you like to write out or pronounce.
words that make you smile or laugh
they can be in any language
don't worry about spelling

_____

_____

_____

_____

_____

_____

_____

_____

_____

_____

_____

Words matter.
They **define**, they **express**, they **create**,
they **evoke**, they **impact**, and certainly **communicate**.
The **words** you use in **your speech**,
the **thoughts** you **learn** and in turn **teach**,
those **syllables** you sounded in **schools**,
are your **utmost powerful** tools.

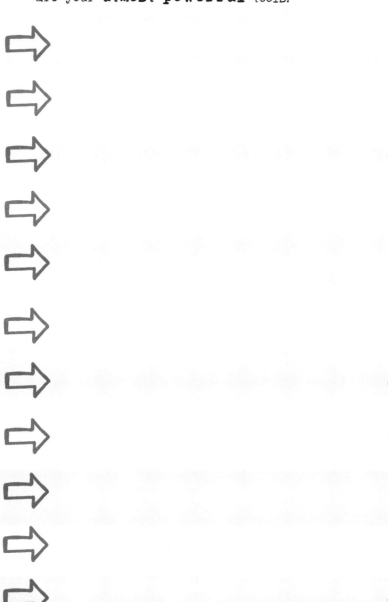

What's **between** the buns?
Lettuce? tomatoes? Some sort of **meat**?
Or will you be **creative**
and draw **something neat?**

You can fill in the space with
whatever you choose.

Maybe you'll **create** a burger
that gets **featured** on the **news.**

Create a billboard you want everyone passing by to see.

What do you Fill your head with?

Draw some stick figures in ACTION!

singing

jumping

Drawing to **music,**
depending on the kind,
can kindly **encourage**
and **stimulate** the mind.
It can **create**
a **blissful meditative** state
or provoke thoughts
and emotionally **exhilarate.**

A **world** of two **arts**
dancing in bond,
yet allowing **you** to freshly
and **freely** respond.

Song:
Artist:
Mood:
Date:

life is like a fish bowl,
keep it clean.

Your influences help **create**
and **shape** who you are.
It's for you to decide who and
what those **influences** are.
It's **good** to know where
your **guidance** comes from
and how it influences
who you become.

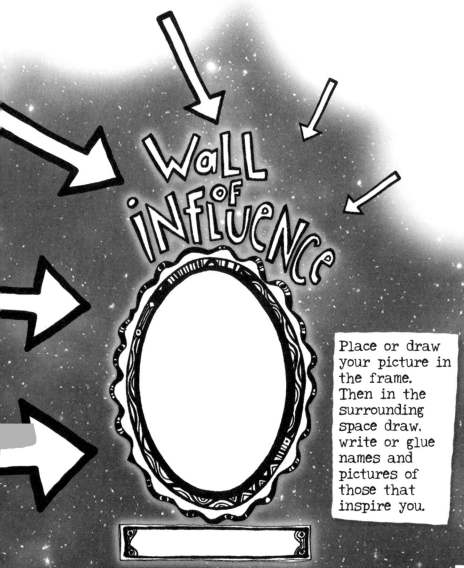

Wall of Influence

Place or draw your picture in the frame. Then in the surrounding space draw, write or glue names and pictures of those that inspire you.

DRAW ONE MOMENT FROM YESTERDAY ↓ ↓ ↓

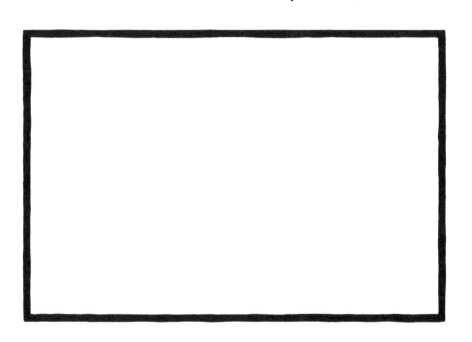

Practicing something like
this with your **mind**,
be it in **your head**,
in **writing** or both combined,
allow parts of your **brain**
to surely **light up**
as you become part
of the **memory club**.

List EVERYTHING you can REMEMBER about YESTERDAY

_____

_____

_____

_____

_____

_____

_____

_____

_____

_____

_____

_____

_____

_____

_____

_____

_____

_____

_____

heads

tails

49

dRAW the complete opposite of a jelly fish

If life had no **opposites**,
would there be any **consequence**?
We've been **taught** about
big and small, left and right,
Open and closed, day and **night.**
But what about a jellyfish
swimming in the lovely **abyss?**
With it no **opposite**
would it begin to **feel** amiss?

(Personality test at neuronsaway.com)

draw a bowl of fruit with your Left hand

In one word how did it make you feel?

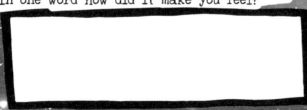

draw a bowl of fruit with your Right hand

In one word how did it make you feel?

Time: something we all religiously live by. But have you ever stopped to **wonder,** what the heck is **time?**

WHAT IS TIME?

WHERE DOES IT COME FROM?

WHERE DOES IT GO?

HOW IMPORTANT IS TIME?

design a t-shirt you'd NEVER, ever wear.

Express your **creations**
right here on this **paper**.
The **creatures** may be similar
to the ones found in **nature.**
Or, they could be an entirely
different **imaginal breed**.
Something like a Pilloflopper,
Caddafan or a **Burblebeede.**

CREATE SOME CREATURES
that Live heRe.

The way you see the world
belongs exclusively to **you.**
This **exercise** strives to show it
from another point of **view.**
Does the **ant** see the grass as
green or the sky just as **blue?**

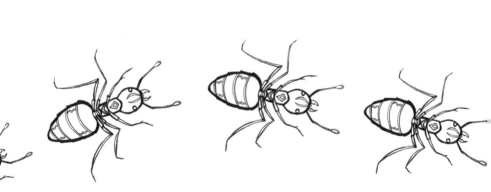

draw what an ANT sees

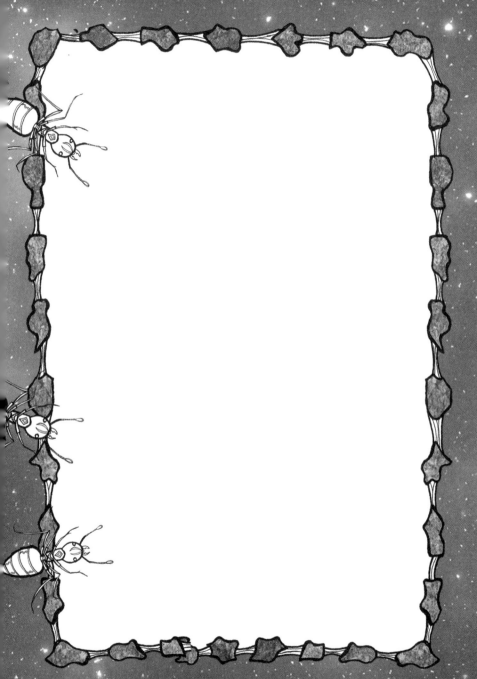

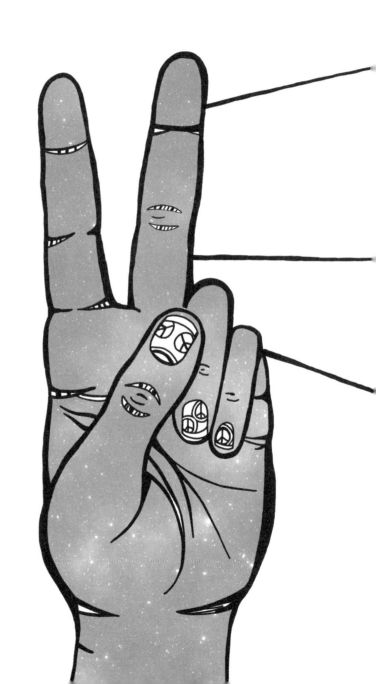

—what is peace? —

—— what can peace do? ——

—how do you create peace?—

What are
8 things you
Love
about yourself?

1.

2.

3.

4.

5.

6.

7.

8.

What's your inner vision?

When you ask the questions
that truly matter
you will find that you
yourself have the answer.
For example:
what does it mean to be free?
It means exactly
what you want it to be.

what does it mean to be free?

Are you free?

How does one become free?

describe or draw your perfect home:

Home is a **space**
where **you** can be **you**
and a **place** you can **share**
with your **loved** ones **too.**
Home is where **you** can
express your own **style**
and you can leave home
every once in **while.**
Home is where
your **Love** abides,
but **home** is truly what
you **feel** on **the inside.**

What are 3 things no one can take away from you?

There are things
that can come and go
and there are things
that can never be let go.
There are things that are
held close to your heart
and there are things
that can easily drift apart.
But only you will ever know
which is which
and only you will ever know
which makes you truly rich.

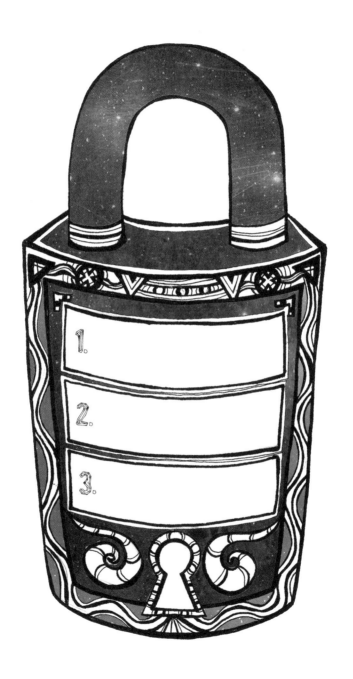

where your attention goes energy flows

Where your very attention goes the energy of existence flows. Your attention is a highly-valued gift; Powerful when focused and idle when adrift. Yet it is you who gets to choose how and why your energy gets used.

what's YOUR attention on?

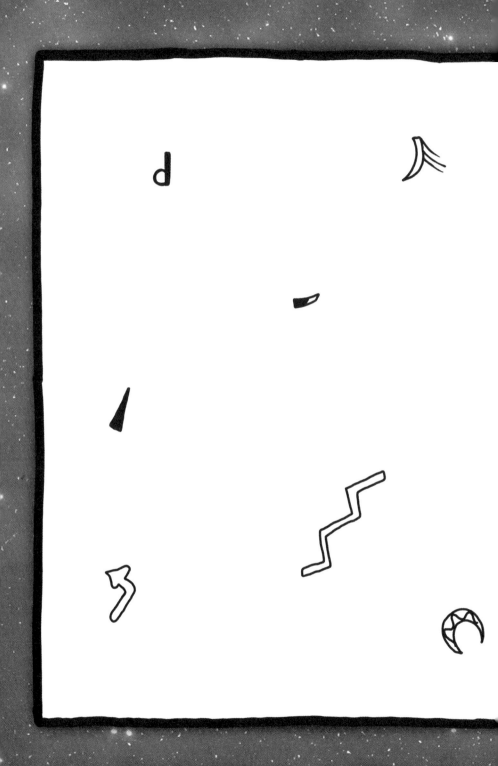

How can **YOU** explain these Colors to Someone **who can't see?**

Do something your future
self will thank you for.

write a letter to yourself ten years from now using your opposite hand.

DeaR

That which you
hold in your heart,
is you.

What's TRULY iN Your heart?

I can _____

I go _____

I hear _____

I think _____

I see _____

I feel _____

I wonder _____

I dream _____

I do _____

I help _____

I hope _____

I love _____

I believe _____

I am _____

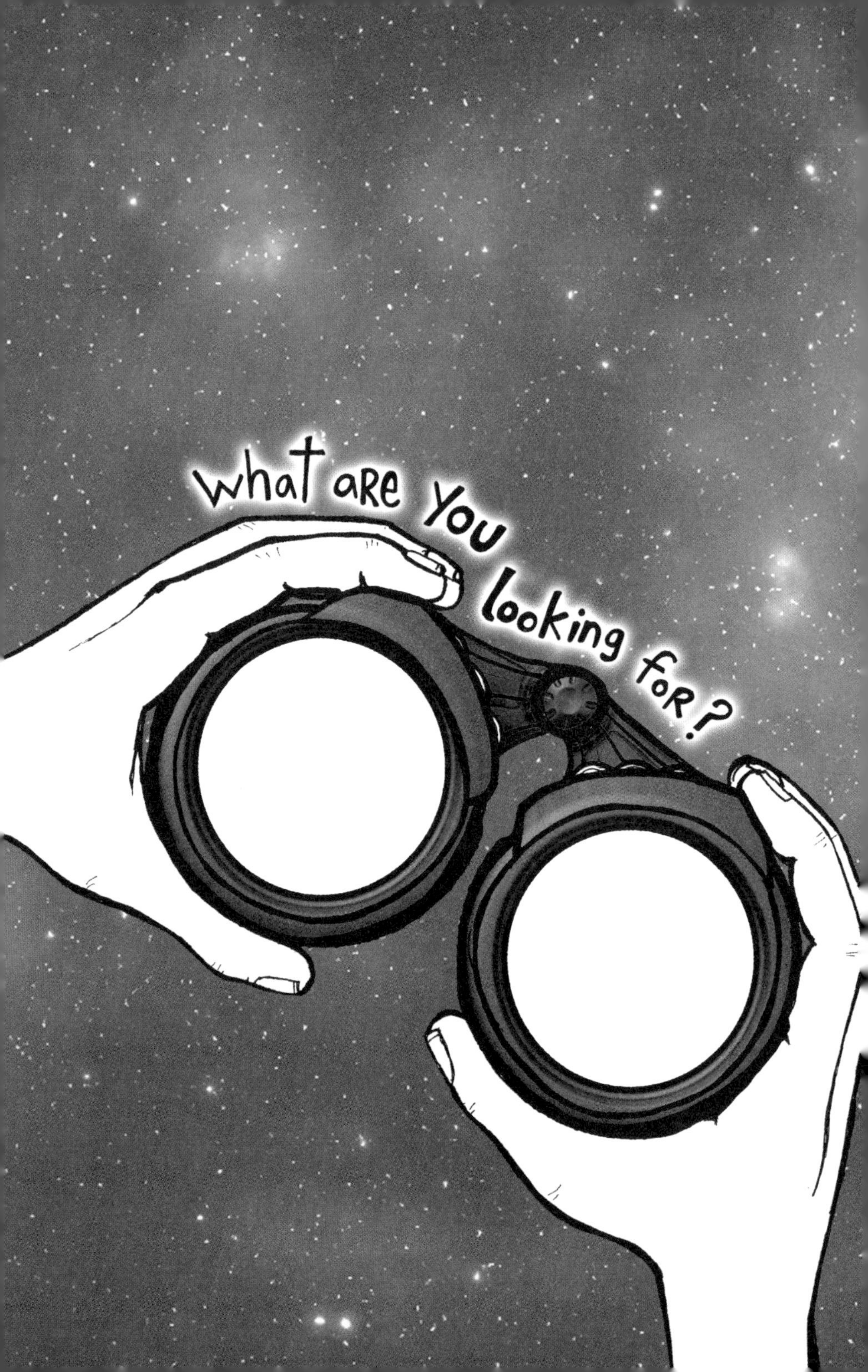
what are you looking for?

We must **respect ourselves**
enough to **walk away**
from the things and people
that lead us an **unkind way.**
We must walk away from the things
that no longer **support** and **nurture us.**
And those that make problems
or continuously cause a big fuss.
It may not seem as **easy** as writing
on a **piece of paper** and tossing it out.
But it is much much **easier**
to live a life without.

What are some of the ways you can remove
those unwanted aspects of your life?

How can you stop them from coming back?

What do You want to Cut Out of Your Life?

(write in the boxes, cut them out and throw them away)

cut here

What's the BEST thing that could happen Today?

_____

_____

_____

_____

_____

_____

There are **things**
that **everyone needs**,
like **sun**, **air**,
water and **seeds**.
But there are **needs** that
are slightly more **personal**
like a favorite teddy bear
or a **writing journal**.
What are the **needs** that **make**
you the **best you can be?**
These are the **needs** that
will set you truly free.

NOTES

NOTES

NOTES